Praise for *Tainted by the Same Counterfeit*

Candice Louisa Daquin's passionately transcendent collection of poems *Tainted by the Same Counterfeit* is a sorcery of language, rich with tight and visceral imagery, filled with summoning and spells, longing and lust, and poems that cut to the bone only to reveal roses blooming from the wounds. It moves through love and geography, through pain and freedom, and reads with a prosody that echoes the Shakespearian in its beauty. This book is the temple and the monk, the blood and the spirit, divine feminine wisdom and the roots of earth's darkness—"the color of aubergine and hibiscus bled in winter river as redwood is lost to time." I am forever tainted by the impressions these poems have pressed upon my psyche.

> —**Kai Coggin**, Author of *Mining for Stardust, Incandescent,* and *Wingspan*

Candice Daquin's poetry provides an exquisite blend of the delicate and powerful, of profound emotion established in simplicity, of eloquence and terror and wisdom born of experience and self-examination. These nuanced and graceful pieces yield insight into the vulnerability of contemporary women; they give us glimpses into grief and longing and the various "forms of starvation and war" so deeply imbedded in our culture. This is an authentic book—a poignant and intense artifact of our times—and one to be treasured.

> —**Robert Okaji**, Author of *My Mother's Ghost Scrubs the Floor at 2 a.m.*

Tainted by the Same Counterfeit is "spectacle and singularity" that swims, dreamlike, through the subconscious, hinting at baryonic matter that disintegrates like a surrealist portrait made of words. The issues of identity and origins, the seeming reality of flesh and fabric, old letters and dog collars, swirls like sea foam on a wintry beach, ultimately leaving nothing but subatomic particles neither from here nor from there, yet rooted , rooted deeply, in loss.

> —**Donna Snyder**, Author & Director of the *Tumblewords Project*

Tainted by the Same Counterfeit is an incredible compilation of raw, vulnerable, palpable poetry from an incomparable writer, well before her time. It is magnetic and pulled me in from start to finish. The words found in these pages will live on in one's mind for years to come; they have lasting power.

> —**Tremaine Loadholt**, Author & Editor, *Medium*

TAINTED BY
THE SAME COUNTERFEIT

poems by

Candice Louisa Daquin

Finishing Line Press
Georgetown, Kentucky

TAINTED BY
THE SAME COUNTERFEIT

Publisher: Leah Huete de Maines
Editor: Christen Kincaid
Cover Art: Fiverr
Author Photo: Candice Louisa Daquin
Cover Design: Maaike Pluym
Interior Illustrations: Monochromier (butterfly image) and Pintal Sari (fox-woman with mask)

Order online: www.finishinglinepress.com
             also available on amazon.com

Author inquiries and mail orders:
Finishing Line Press
P. O. Box 1626
Georgetown, Kentucky 40324
U. S. A.

Table of Contents

This collection of poetry is for those who were there for me when I was sick in 2017. Without you, I would not have survived. I can never thank you enough.

I dedicate this book to the wonderful author, poet & beloved friend—Cordelia Feldman.

"For as long as we live, they too will live, for they are now a part of us as, We remember them." (Jewish prayer)

"Anyone whose goal is "something higher" must expect some day to suffer vertigo. What is vertigo? Fear of falling? Then why do we feel it even when the observation tower comes equipped with a sturdy handrail? No, vertigo is something other than the fear of falling. It is the voice of emptiness below us which tempts and lures us, it is the desire to fall, against which, terrified, we defend ourselves."

      Milan Kundera, *The Unbearable Lightness of Being*

"*Le réel ...n'attend rien de la parole.*"

      —Jacques Lacan, Psychoanalyst, *Ecrits*

TAINTED BY
THE SAME COUNTERFEIT

The memory of clothes

Somewhere in a filing room with corrugated cardboard and dried blood
her skirt of 2006 is folded by a uniformed man
who isn't used to folding women's clothes.
She'll not be wearing it again
it's evidence of a crime committed
of a bad start and a hundred reasons why
gut instinct should be heeded
something she didn't know back then—
packing and unpacking
the accoutrements of a life
worn a little faded and down in the heel.

Some days she'd sleep
in your oversized rock concert T-shirt
smelling the distant indifference of your brand of love
others, it'd be the outline of a coat hung in hallway
reminding her of nightmares she thought left behind.

Wherever you go, there you are
the psychology majors chimed in falsetto chorus—
they didn't know she was running, because she was so versed at standing in place
"Cheese" Smile for the camera, the pedophile said
that day she wore a pink beret and she's always worn hats—
to disguise herself from her own scrutiny.
You liked those scarlet hose and how her underwear didn't match
you even liked the outline she left in your well-worn yellow bedsheets.

Despite that, she's a ghost
wearing hand-me-down clothes without labels
posing in storefronts
for feelings dipped in formaldehyde.

If she could step into a time machine
she'd escape her own bad tempo
retreating to a distant past
where the clothes she wore
carried no memory

or voices scolding over radio wave—
like a diver unable to exclaim aloud
when the white whale comes into view.

That's all she sees sometimes
outlines, shadows and snuff stinging her eyes
snapshots of who she was, before
the picture was over-exposed.

There she is—
running breathless down a stony beach
toward nothing and no-one and still
there's a peace in her eyes that's absent, she makes up for
with midnight blue and eighties pink
just like kids who paint their dolls and dress them
ready to begin a new game
never considering what happens
on the other side of starting over.

They sell her size by the dozen
and other women wear it well
she's ready to dissolve to the bottom
like malt and sugar stirs with mint
and creates momentary confusion
is it sweet?
Or is it bitter?

Try her on
she's a glove that may fit
or maybe
your fingers will be too short, too long
your palm a might too thick—
with her Pantone of regret.

La politique de la chaise vide

Two chairs
pull toward each other
as if in tilt, they possess animation
capable of strung attachment
emotion usually ascribed humans
though as I observe the land
coarse in hominid season
like imperfect viola pulled heavily with specious string
it is a faultless metaphor
I'll have your guts for garters
so sayeth the oscillating planet
fierce in polished destiny.

Perhaps we are given, too much
expecting our quivering hearts
to do justice to goodness
capable of capturing brush of silence, tracked quietly in kitchen
after hours, a low throated clock
fragile light spilling against
two chairs, reaching in rent
emotion, a scant too statuary for
complete touch.

Relinquished habits

Deep below the earth
I might have found you
climbing from stalagmites
brushed in clay

there's a cost for
relinquished habits
bowing in bad weather
until warp sets in.

The rule curve

A dream reminded me of that winter
snowed in house, cut off from sound
ice storm and horror movies
kurt cobain, everyone wearing plaid
stringy hair and grinding hips
the rat eating his cardboard house
you smoking in velvet chair
sundays interminable release from despair
the glimmering portent of future—
hope of youth, our beautiful torment
all is possible, nothing as real as it feels
the illusion and persistence of dreams
did I sleep, to wake 20 years hence?
Still thinking tomorrow, I will sit exams
anxious briefly, as if time were a rubber band
no more the rule and curve of outstretched hands
before we could afford tattoos, dyeing our hair with fragments
only the gentle footfall of sex and orange light bulbs
swinging like marmalade, choices made and made not
kissing arbitrary strangers at costume parties
we drive crowded in steamed up cars
disguising our zeal behind fogged windows
you pull over for a piss, I run out into empty fields
legs scratched by dead corn; the sky looks enormous
in a rush of past and future, myself in reflection
staring upward, do I know then what will come to pass?
Would it make any difference? or are we part of a greater weave?
Rushing to the culmination of ourselves, only to look back retreating?
Far through time, changing lens, adding dilution and tint
until the picture we held once in our tight skin
becomes the us of now, solidified in our weft
like a tree feels its way deep into soil
grasping blindly for roots
to feed.

The Opal

I think of you
my heart clenches
in the carousel of seconds, it takes to form a moment, yet I managed to witness
    a lifetime
how did you come to be?
a vowel, a constellation, a rhyme in my mind
days are bare, unpainted walls
thinking of you; I find color, music
I want to breathe you in—
molecules and seconds
making up days spent together, pieces of paper forming a page
marbles inside the other
flowers retaining pigment as they dry
death and life, striding side by side
dancing beneath raw bulb, open sky
the pulse in your throat, the clench of your thigh
sweetness in a certain, slow agony
instrument run over temperate string
the cry of unseen things in dark
listen, listen, closer, I bend my head
you tell me everything in one pearlized glance
if there were a creature able to step from shell, made flesh
I think she'd be you; you with your untouchable countenance
the regal surety of your long sloping neckline
how cheek bones become canvas, become art, become song
your chest against mine, just once, like a film played forward and backwards
I see the embrace, an awkwardness, then I'm wearing my best dress, nearly
    spent, bare feet on dirty street roads, because I wore heals to look like your
    fantasy and one broke clean in half

you can take things like that as omens
I'll continue to believe where there are feelings, there are destinations
electricity above us in the heavens, sprung to earth
lines in sand, in skin, in the consoling sky at night
across your sleeping form, when I want you to dream like i
building on fantasy, stories come fully real
only in others' lives it seems, you swim ever further away

until a shadow, a mirage, just the sound of your escape
sometimes you strangle the moment, with accident or heavy hand
intensity not meant for now, should take its time to build
I gave you no time; in my world you had long been its center
a flower within flowers, mandala tattooed on the small of my back in purple,
    calling

I think of you
my heart clenches
in the carousel of seconds, it takes to form a moment, yet I managed to witness
    a lifetime
before the end there was a beginning, unsung, untested, disused, scythed baren
leaving nothing in its scatter but wistfulness
like a memory without basis, not existing, just as real

the feel of your reddened lips, goodbye, never touched, still here
in the unfolding of time, you flicker closer, then far, then in, then
out
like an opal on my finger
luminous, unforgettable, the night air charged with its curse.

Let it out

The match you struck
leaves its sulfur
like slept on sheets
retain outline
of lovers
who before morning, must rise
shake off their reverie and hope
for life containing pleasure and warmth
submerging in cold water
become once again, closed faced
workers in suckled world
with cast heads, staring at concrete floor
whilst cats above
on roof tops
cry to one another
sounding much like
ourselves, if we were to
just
let it out.

This time will come again

The saw they used—
had teeth like rabbits, unaware
they were herbivores
her shell broke
like a blue egg
on turpentine floor
for the ants to summon
their legions and devour
she could smell her own fall
by the pinch of their envy
though why anyone should—
be jealous, she found absurd
as plates will chip
when placed on top of one another
we leave the best for last
scouring our hides with vinegar
all the holy and the ivory
thrown in pyre to await defeat
she tried to tell them
it's not me you want
it's yourselves
the competition is within
I am nothing
but a representation
the dreaming void
or lost moon, reflecting your own
do not bury me with nightshade
violet black on my tongue
or strangle my words, because you have none
this time will come again
as all circles are undone and reknotted
by fate and the scepter
in the wrists of those
cutting down trees who only seek
the silence of being above
cacophony of rude arrows

felling our roots
though we strive
only
to master ourselves.

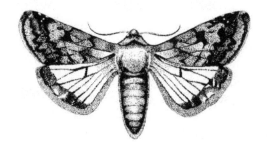

The cure

The poison
was the medicine
the medicine
was the sickness
the sickness
killed her
without it—
she could not live.

Pretending to stand still

The doctor said
straighten your shoulders
your back is becoming curved
I told him
that may not be possible
time permitting
I have a train to catch
I need to walk on all fours
and pretend to be a lion
he wrote me a script—
for fierceness
I handed it in to the pharmacist
who clicked her tongue
rolled her eyes
a little like a deer who is trying
to look sideways at
approaching foe
whilst pretending to
stand still.

(First published in cuckoo in crisis, poems by 25 women poets,
Akhand publishing house)

Hymen

Too soon
the child menstruates
bleeding away her right to play
she is captured behind glass
starched and polished
until catching eye of man
old enough to have given her life
she is sold
some marriages are not proper choices
even as she signs her name
for later, her private parts are laid bare
under a shard of glass, standing in for knife
then the girl knows
she is a woman
spreading her wide, to ensure she was not defiled
her hymen reinforced, clitoris removed
fearing, if she is not sewn tightly enough
her husband will not feel special, nor soak the ritual bed sheet
scarlet
she could die, if she does not tear apart
sufficiently for the relatives
who bay for her blood, fearing
if she feels anything, but gratitude and pain
she may be tempted by someone else
perhaps a boy her own age
who with her in the dirt played
before she had to give up
being a child and become
a woman slain
in shackles of faith.

Metallurgical

Exposure
last decibel
falling off my shoulders
unhook my poetry
before dementia settles
her furred cap
running down my legs
cedar season
main character for a
wreckage
read by weak light
hoist our innards
buckets of guts
soup for the cold
that never comes
I can press my breasts
against you until they lie flat
feeling your heart race
between us
turning in delivered poise
let lose my secrets

I'd dress in nails for you
go on, just test

my metal.

The dusk of us

Our bed is no bed at all
for I sleep running
and in dusk
grind molars out
to vaporize
as nightmares wink
savage play

waking or woken
never entirely full
often empty
that cold 1930s tile
a blue I hate
insipid like stewed, savage tea
given when ill
makes you capture retch
behind feign of wrist

we
sink
I forget how to breathe
soon
sleep and
that wakeful state
shall in conspiracy
dominate no
more than
a stray
thought
caught
the dusk of us
tearing on
this
barbed
wind.

Let go and take flight

He said
I would have dated you twenty years ago
it struck me ... time has skates
but they are not my feet in them
a girl like the pin-up on the cars l.p., cover
wizzes past, talking in modern languages, I seem to have closed my ears to

all of a sudden, paraphrasing life seems to come with tags
numbers for when you can't, and when you can:
18 you can show me your tits
40 I don't want to see them
20 you can wear thigh-high-socks and miniskirts
45 you shouldn't wear brightly colored lipstick
as if times wick, were burning in another room

as you sit down for dinner, musing over the day
as next-door life runs away, we age out of sight
growing snaggle toothed in the eyes of labels conferred
rules abject and constraining

like the drawers of our parents, we looked in as a child
always wondering, how do they not have time to go through this stuff?
How can a ten-year-old letter still be here?
Or pictures of my mom wearing a bra, my dad with his favorite car, an old
collar belonging to the dog bones in the garden

for a child, time is unfathomed, they stare intensely, every day a ring in the tree to
study
grown, we turn away and soon, those drawers are overflowing
valentine's from 15 years ago, old pots of cold cream, notes on fraying paper
lost, reclaimed, achingly familiar and strange

now is a wind obliterating thought
gusting forward, inevitable sycophant
we are riding on our own coat tails
those who remain bright
let go and take
flight.

That we were clay

Oh women
we live in a western mirage
where fantastic stories of weight loss
garner 1000 likes and uplifting
botox dreams permeate lash studios

infrequently we cry at real things
but we judge the homeless woman who asks for money at traffic lights
and feel we've given when we tithe
not remembering our march in 1977

women's year; why do we need a year?
When did we stop pulling others up behind us?
Instead of mending broken ceilings shut?
Haven't we cracked the glass? Isn't it
cool to be cleaning, bringing up kids, having great sex, a career, holding down
    the fort
march for susan komen, staying thin on diet cola
don't we have it all?
Why have it all?

Oh women
where are our sisters?
Where the tender nurture?
Where skin without muscle?

Oh women
slow down
disease chases those who survive by drowning
stop and listen to the beat of your heart
far from competitive playground

teach your daughters to dream
not weight loss and prom dresses
nor crabs in a bucket, pinching others back
that we emerged from clay
forging and set, with our tender strength
each other free.

Undone in spectacle and singularity

Vying the night, when against a single bulb, it holds no answers but emptiness, come of sleeplessness and waste, flotsoming down dirt strewn roads, where wind will not go.

We know of no other way but self-destruction. Our arms bear witness to the predilection; even paper, a wane thing, crumples in our presence. We crease sheets with worn emotion, and wrap the rest of our fleshy hearts in newsprint, only nobody reads newspapers, they glide through windows like mechanical birds and I masturbate to daylight as you try to swallow normal with your morning vitamin.

We are not of this place; we didn't come from here. We came from starlight and forgotten pasts, flickering like tiger moths against freshly painted walls. If we stick too long, our legs will be ripped off and we'll fall, catching lime colored glass of window panes, in our echo to oblivion, and lie upside down in dirty sunlight turning to dust. Baryonic matter, capturing descent in abseil, watchful, watchful ever soft, in hushed float.

The bee flying in behind us, he died too. Never to make honey again, nor feel on his fur, that warmth come of freedom. We, all struck by illusion too thick for breath, wings like melting thimbles of glass, bodies as confectionery, light as confession, borne of a pure heart. You unzip your secrets, they pour like treacle into my hair, and we come together.

I pull you through fear

Find my hand
reaching down into water well
where sides are round and l am hollow
filled by intermittent pulse
causing your existence
to blossom within wasteland

before, I saw nothing
noise was chalk, silence, a glassy lake
the boat frozen in dying reeds
you were the pith in my step
before you, I had forgotten to breathe

let me suspend to safer shore
pull you through fear
as disease rattles her terrors
find my hand
in oblique shift of destinies
grown strong on your steady gaze
I reach
catching your fall
and hold you up
out of harm
no end of us
we own our flight
sweeping like reddening brushstroke
pollinating everywhere
we live.

We, made of paper

We
made of paper
write our words
in careful ink
watching how
underside bleeds

we
made of
fog
obscure our
walk forward
in obstacle
and loss

we
made of
wrung hands
gather yet, dry clothes on line
before rain, unbidden
falls in noiseless sheets
turning lawn
vivid green

we
made of
incomplete stitch
find no substance within
wicked light
dashes birds from roost
darkening impending cloud
like spilt ink
the words
of stained radiance
dried and smudge proof.

Only a glove

I think it was
my glove they found
by the edge of the sea
I think it was
my tears that stained it
with a different salt
from inside
this empty beach
washing up grief

does it get easier to
examine the shell of your life
wondering how you built
such transparent castles?
How hollow they sound
walking through, in pointed shoes
so different to the inside
of you
crying out for
something other
than this physical
abyss

be real then, have shape
exist
surely not everything
is a filing draw
chore
work
certificate of life
by collecting
those times
we ascend

reaching for
shells
through water

though cold
our feet bare
now unable to make out if they
underneath
are still there
whitened reminder against sand
of similar stilted
lives

my glove lost, as you were
no more a reality
than those
shimmering lines
we walk upon
unknowing
admiring beach, sea
never once imagining
this could be me
this could be me
washed up shore
infinite, misplaced
in glittering distance
only a glove
smelling of loss.

New Hampshire

We
territories of heart
take for granted
even
pain

encircling the
recess of spite
we bow to
flame
little morsels
who
with rapacious
lust
devour
the emptiness

pain is a worn demon
sitting down for dinner
we eat
in formation
saving knife for last

pain is an open attic window
knocking against wind
flung by what?
We don't admit
to bang and wake
silence within

pain, golden apple
pair of shoes
we ride so swiftly on
her back
it doesn't feel
sharp.

Intimidation

True intimidation isn't deliberate—
it's the way others see you
even when you have no agenda
within you, a power they perceive
perhaps you just have nothing left—
to lose
take me as I am—
damn it
or set me free
of social rule

we play the game when young
comb your hair
wear a smile
don't let your buttons come undone
grin for camera
snap
put your shoulders back
legs together
legs apart
we play our part

as age demolishes hunger
as skinned, we clamber for succor
intimidation is our art
chained inside
fire escapes our eyes
one look
one grazed gaze
we purchase pieces of costume
rev up the game
dinner eats the diner
let's turn form on its head
and dance barefoot, deft
learned in bondaged war
with ourselves.

Nourishment

I am a soul needing
nourishment
it does
not come in usual
form
used to
chain and ball

I am a light-footed girl
born in helium
it is not my path
to be shackled
by spirit & lead road

you may like your
comfortable idling
warm radiator
closed windows
tin heart
the doors stapled
floor wet
with apathy

you grasp
my wings
tie them
to ordinary
things
taking vowels
out of oceans

I am unable to
stay tethered
by saturday shop
and monday drop off
walking dead
cubicle crow

please
understand
if air were
sucked from
your marrow
I would lend
life
bid you escape
cage and seek
shimmer in night

do
not
condemn
me
my restlessness
I was
never
here
I am
just
flame
on fringe
of curtailed
theatre.

Then when I do

Taking the long way home, under blackberry bower
left by a year of growing over
and the clay pigeon shed, tiny broken windows, the smell
of musty activity, spiders bid for space and hang their imagination
from perishing rafters
places you and I have been
to dissolve the salt of the day
in each other's mouths
tasting tears, sweat, frustration
like chilled drinks rowed on a bar
different colors
shades of the same
your face is bent with laughing
mine is blotchy from drinking
and yet you hold it so dearly
touching my skin
as if it were your own.

Crocus of their heart

You found me on the edge of the world
where only tumbleweed and lost directions fell
spilling into chasm, rendering fallow
land uninhabited by those striving to untender yen
you gathered me into your warmth
as dazed wood pheasant, is saved by speeding motorist
guilty in his luxury, he bends to undo damage
rent on broken wing by metal pursuit
in dim light I repaired, against your effort
like deer grown in forest, spring at first dawn
when light finds space and green darkness calls home
electrifying their urge to sprint beyond their origin
I had given up thinking anyone would reach me
and there you were
an unexpected claim upon my chilled static
revealing spell of all who pretend to cease
when beneath loss, lies all along …
the crocus of their heart.

Falling into sync

The first time I fell
you picked me up and dusted me off
there, there, it isn't bleeding badly
can you stand? where does it hurt?
And skating away into the circle of
other jacketed figures swirling in unison
you were gone
and i—
I hurt
unable to locate
origin

the second time I fell
you had been buying something from a street vendor
the car doors opened with such swiftness
I didn't see anyone scoop me up and drive off
but somehow, I was no longer there
waiting for you to turn around, arms full of
purchase

the third time I fell
was into darkness and I couldn't see
my way out
the room confined anguish like a corset
life did not seem worthy of acknowledgement
I had vanquished my taste for living
that's what happens when
the quill of an arrow-head
is laced with careful poison

the last time I fell
your hands were on my forehead
I burned like an unsaid emotion, ready to cease
in the morning. we rose again, together
to

try this thing of living
because you
refused to
give up
on me.

Is it you?

Is it you?
who woke me this morning
lying hot in sleep
is it you?
Who bathed me, hiding my bruises from light
keeping warm water, running in my ears
is it you?
who tells me all I fear, is fear itself
and makes of life, this funny puppet show
ritual, bandage, death
living is just guessed
is it you?
Keeps me whole
wants to bring me back again
though I do not want to go, out of my shell
painted and green, hidden among garden gnomes
little lies, little trials. is it you?
Keeps making me smile?

How a child, how a man

The brightest of the church
irregular, long pointed cross, feels handmade in irregularity
so light despite small window, the red almost electric
they look so indistinct against such a backdrop
torn chunks of wet melon, darkening earth, sweet and ragged
a white dress, lace over lace, thin fabric, silhouette within summit,
her long neck, a letter dipped in coffee
saffron seeds blown urgently, burying their dry tips in aubergine earth
a black cross, lacquered and shiny, quenched in chalky frame,
the only shadow against mesa of ruby
he keeps his head down, seeing with closed eyes her mahogany lips, open
slightly in effort, lighting candles with soft bend, a fan, folding in parts like a
map of the world
her fingers will taste of lime, salt and coal. her eyes onyx almonds closed against
chaffing stain of obedience

Study patience, mark time in fevered listing, whet appetite against stillness.
Here, there is your reward. Still briny from journeying, her legs shaking him
out into your arms, so it is, so she prays. Tightly into statues, looking into light.
How a child, how a man, nine turns of moon, humble against her creationism,
endeavors gratitude in absolution of ego.

Explaining silent love

And if it was for you
sitting in the wrong seat
saying the right things
reversal of fortune
among the lilies of the discrete
we communicate between sentences
speaking in tongues, in darkness
of a thought before it's freed
and it was for you
all along—
no wonder.

Shaking hands with beginning

You stood over me
a repository of untapped energy
sleep by hades
damnable spitting, quiet night

first time alone
you will grow familiar with time
fade again as we break apart
cherry and its stone
I retain the core of you
where sweet juice is strongest

that elemental *bollinger*
worming insistent
shadow's lark, erasable in stillness
splitting air, hands in water
tugging me to surface

mouth of fruit, red juice
bleeding each other's consent
shredded halves regaining
certainty in seed

we feed on this saturated
cloth, redolent in fracture
no longer certain
time, place, intent
applies to mauled movement
rending pieces, divisible into one

seamless place
within, without
solace for structure
untenable, inviolate
racing hares
quivered by
puncture.

Tempest

Give me a role, I'll show you the rote
yet in sulphur we surface to meld with our mold
suzanne is a healer, she lends broken bones wholeness
al makes iron from the pitch of his tongue
claro dices fields with risk laden crops
jonas makes measure and builds us a home
but what does imogen do?
when she is born, the midwives inspect her,
fingers remain shut, her placid face serene, and they say

she doesn't cry, she had no competition in her

she doesn't smile, so she won't be a popular breeder

she hasn't kicked, so her feet aren't strong for forging

her fingers too short, she'll not weave us clothes

her eyes squint, she may not forage for acorns, herbs and blackcurrants

they hold her thin frame to the light like a dazzled albino bat
she has the fire of an outsider in her breath, measure she gauges in abacus
    detachment
the eyes of a questioner, the temper of a divider
she'll sit in darkness and think, the word of man whispered in soot
she is the speaker of unspoken things, her die is cast, sorrow it will become

every generation
a child born
lives to tell
the chicory melancholy of our lives
not distracted by earthly swell nor joyous ritual, they remain unmoved by usual
things
a witness to life and its myriad tragedies
taking turn, each family born, a darkling of no discernible light
she is the night; she cleaved in shadow, no quenched closure to sorrows mantle
standing upright in tilting tempest

perhaps you know her?

Here the children

Here the bell
lowing in pasture
here the children
slouching in classroom

we remember few sums, more of
how it felt un-wrinkling in furtive scoop
love letters in the making
smudged ink, badly drawn cartoon
how we longed for favor

surly and confident on self-made throne
king of the school ground
our ill formed bust, freckles, high forehead, thin legs, gymnasts hips
no enticement for thirteen-year-old boys stuck in id

once at a sleep over, spinning bottles with scarlet-cheeked terror
we fumbled in cupboard, the smell of strawberry tobacco
face as smooth as mine, a hardness below the waist
for the girl who wasn't picked
waiting cross-legged for us to finish and have her chance

the night was cold and hollow hearted
when I learned early
who we like, is often not returned
as story books said; fitting slippers, climbing kissers
it seemed cruel to spar with boys searching for c-cups

if only then, given thought
to the absurdity of one-way infatuation
our conflated adolescence
scurry of petting, tinged with hungover regret

brightening bare trees
youth's folly, become weary-eyed
countenance, walking long paths in abeyance
until when you stop searching, they find you

open your stitches, climb in
inhabiting what had turned cold, in natural turn
as if you were never
awkward
or last choice.

Loathe

We, who are loathe to confess our sins
sleep in helmets on the edge of the world
observing with dismay, those who disregard conscience.

Mailed in pieces

There is a hole in your envelope
where your letter lies folded
meaning has slipped
out
leaving behind
less clarity
I turn over
to see your handwriting
soft ink swirls, unfamiliar and known
you're trying to communicate
across our distance

"listen to me!" you beckon
"I'm the one who
curling my t's and r's
tried to demonstrate
with smudge and blot
configured into written shapes
landscape of my heart"

though ever a sucker for
effort and postage stamp
it strikes dull against ancient armor
you see …
when letters were in vogue
I was queen of paper and felt
my post box swelled with suitors who had
learned the kerning of words
my standards, though I try not to let it show
far higher than, pretty paper and violet pen

this isn't personal
but they trapped the moon for me
left my thighs damp with expression
and you? you missed the rush

of my youth passing through
where doors swung
open in invite
now form letters in
glue.

Après Vous

As quickly as a shoal of thoughts spilling into sunset
knock, knock
warm rain pours like treacle
your hair reminds me of a skull cap of pitch
glinting under a winking red moon
fingering the cobwebs of starlight in urgent betrothal
we dance
we touch
as quickly as a shoal of thoughts spilling into sunset
after me, *après vous*

as stealthfully as a summer's sudden theatrical thunder
knock, knock
life is fidgeting outside, bursting at the seams
wearing her saffron dress with sequins, whirling under chestnut trees
heaving with expectant bosoms and light hearts
you kiss
I return it
as stealthfully as summer's sudden theatrical thunder
after me, *après vous*.

Rubber stamps

Did you send a letter?
that sat on the ledge until it was thrown away, accidently with other unwanted
    things?
What did it say?
Did you apologize for leaving me pregnant? for hitting until I fell
the crack of my head resounding, against your expensive green tile
did you write it in my blood?
With the lies you spun as quill?
Tell me, if I lay with you
you'd, you'd, you'd
fuck me with love rather than rubber?
Did you send me a letter?
That sat on the ledge until it was thrown away, accidentally with other unwanted
    things?
What did it say?

Quickening in want

Fat seed lay its life between thighs
lamp rubbed, quickened
skin hardly cooled in puzzled waiver
he caught my hips in palm
curious sum
of composed energy
shaking his intention deep
leaving shame, an uneven seam

I grew outward, floating tea
expanding in hot water
my cheeks felt hot
you kicked me with narrow arrow
pierced my heart, little one,
attached in truth we lay,
watching rain
until swallowed swirl
cream in coffee
abandoned slippers
blood on handle

no
not you
too

phone rang in perpetuity
shrill song bird to
emptying womb
she would not thrive
in my cradled need
nor grow to become
a mirror
different in echoing
stir

when did you climb?
Inside the core of my part

staying there when blood ran
hot rivers of crimson
voice of conscience and child
unmaterialized

step on water's edge
wet stone, thin ankles
gather strength
you walk in my print
a red finger, pointing in

leaves turn russet, fall
old dancers assessing ends
like faded chorus finishes
closing piano
my breasts, loose questions
empty, drooping
your breathing ceased
reminder of
loss in timbered road
a mark of where you flew
over me, whole, and translucent

those who touched my
chest as lovers, remarked
for one so young
what cause ascribed
this premature sag?

And a wrinkle
like gathered curtain
drowsy with recollection
said nothing audible in response
as creasing
I smiled
in
want.

Honor

Honor
you are a thing best pressed flat, beneath forgetful slats
do not appear and mock
my bare footed lack of
it wasn't I who began
to defile myself nor
when they lined up and I nailed myself
it's not always easy to tell
when the crime begot the criminal
or how the break is sometimes the very thing
you return to again and again
running your fingers down well-worn cracks
here! Fill it with gold, nay! Fill it with lead
somewhere on the metallurgic table of
elements
drown yourself with good intention
what is precious? What easily taken?
Ladies are primroses, lasting just a season
bright like lipstick worn by a dowdy heart
seeking to alight in redemptive plait
weave yourself back into the story
I did not need to apply salve or solution
to garner night-time attention
it came before I knew its chiseled name
in the fingers and the undone buttons of
pain bottled by shaking hands
they swig their lurching tempers
they stomp their ashen parents
into dust for they are not much
more than living rust
growing barnacles and shame by the wet pound
and I never knew
what it felt like to be proud
of my purity which hadn't lasted into summer
nor the taint I grew to shape
into tempting cool drinks
sweating out the last of their

exposure under the scold of impatient heat
that loss of honor so definite
a mark on your brow, marring those who look
before ever, you speak a word of truth
none needed against rude assume
leathery in age, easier for the judge
to sear a girl for outlasting
their cored and pared
fruiting rage.

Home

Throw light on tableau
stark, our characters form reluctant worms
choosing well-worn path
harder to divine from recoil, that bridge
elastic in space like rubber bands
little girls elongate, yearning in fantasy
hopscotched into their roles
white sheet, yet stained with after birth
hair brushed back; we face ourselves at scarred tables
one carries a switch of hazel, tells of easing pain
whilst other languishes on IV
hear the drip of their remedy, seeking trance
to be removed from this blister and lance themselves
from watch of brethren as they fall
matchsticks tindering against time's low bell
who shall seek cliffs edge? Who gentle swell
of rain meeting sea, all washed oblique
no beginning in our rinse
this cloud covers nothing, but a wish to be everlasting
knowing our claim will devour
make then, in this needy wrap of night
muscular in her prowl
my opening mouth on yours, searching for equity
we writhe in our need to exist
when those around us weakly cease
some say death brings us closer
sexing in cupboards by the mortuary
sign in, take a seat, cast your clothes
one step removed from beasts, our burden
knowing as witnesses, we plunder fear in earthbound sweat and tears
you break over me, splintering your hunger
against my yielding warmth, we are two children
lost in the spilt comfort of utero, searching for brothers, like lighthouses
blushing against whisper of fog, blot in and out, a morse code
decipher my loins, slick with damage
rest your aching in my enveloping bondage
tied by the neck, to hang like December rabbits lacking escape

we are the warmth of apple sauce and spice
lost on haunted tongue, fugitives meeting in fear
entwining bloodied fingers, we forge moonshine and defy calculation
all who live, must cease in their turn
as knowing, we buck against fate
brandishing longing for one more sip of comfort, laid loving on our brow
before seasons shift like weary walkers, hunched against cold
breaking whiteness of fields
flushed, longing to reach home.

Fox

Drag me out of the lake
before it ices
pull my recalcitrant arms
out of their doll sockets
pop pop
goes the farmer's gun
hush little rabbits
don't make a sound
blood is russet against wire
you scrape me void
embed the need
we spin in crystallized catkin
my dress is smothering your
bad notion
starve out the longing
makes you so evil
green glass raised to
moon without
give me one sharp pinch
wake without prince's touch
water logged
heavy to the touch
too fast in spin
blackness is a blot of goodness
on the tip of my finger
swallow me
I'm intoxicate
I'll wake you from the drum
beat you heady into rhythm
let's jostle for position
ending up rubric on well-worn floor
here the songs consume me
follow the leader
all fall down
watch blooming plague taste our spite
survivors don't speak loudly
hush

I'm so heavy
with the seed you've sewn
I could burn
red as a fox
cast in snarl.

Constellations

A list exists
of all the addresses, of all the people I have ever known
well enough to remember
a list like a map of constellations
pointing in myriad direction
if you go this way and lie underneath the lilac tree
you will grow long white roots
if you choose another path, the one where orange soil
burns the soles of your feet
you may never return
and if you choose to fling
yourself from the rocks of Cyprus
into a green sea
you may see the magnification of the world
through your veins
already we know the choices we will make
what lies impossible for us
drying out starfish, pressing against sand
may seem like an option but
everything is preordained before we know
as if some guiding hand
moves us sundering toward the end
with gentle entreaty
I could have told you at seven years old
what I would have done and those things
better left for dare-devils who Rollerblade closer to the sun
I could have written out my sum and all its stars
and made of the paper, a map
of my journey before, indeed
I knew the meaning of such quest
as the girl who sits out the game
thinking of faraway places, instead of pursuit
or she who climbed the tallest tree knows
this will not confine her hunger
at such tender ages, we become the calculation of ourselves
I was always wearing costumes, left over from school play
when it came time to remove my mask and my tail

I found it melancholy to return to ordinary
as others seek riches, or know how to surf highest wave
fearless in their far-flung gaze
I knew the edge of the lake
was as far as I would dare step
without looking back, without some regret
and nothing and no one changes so much
they cannot find
their way back.

Common denominator

She was curious
I was jaded
alcohol
common denominator
she tried hard
I pitied her effort
imagining a man
slamming her against outside wall
I'll take your effort and
leave you raw
no that's not how a lady
behaves I thought
opening her car door
we drove in silence
to her bi-curious flat
she had pictures of men
with muscular chests
and photos of her cat
on the empty fridge
where straight girls purge
and drink minerals but never
sugar
they are
already too sweet
she opened like a lotus
lying like a star
in a carpet of darkness
I taught her why
stereotypes lie
my bra more lacy
my panties more racy
my heels sharper
I lifted her out
of her little mold
and made her cry out
like she was a new-born
she whispered

I didn't know it could be
so good
I have always been sure, I said
Pawn takes Queen
let me pour you another
shot of me.

Gravity

Sitting in thin chairs on street walk
in the south of France
they don't wear bras
my male companion attempts, vainly
to close his mouth
I tell him; *wait until you get to the beach*
he shifts uncomfortably in his damp seat
I tilt my head back to take in a lungful of sun
and a drag of my *Gauloises*
because life then, is humorous, if not good
interesting, if not safe, sorrowful, rather than empty
watching boys become men, their stiffening intention
before sharp rocks tear apart
and everyone goes under water
he will one day have his little heart
scolded by a model
with aspirin tits and a G-string
the size of my toothpick
he will not play in his band past 25
preferring to nurse the delights of easy drugs
and girls with five-inch stilettos
and I, will freckle and eventually burn
underneath the skirt of summer
where fine lines will form around my puckered mouth
and I will taste their use of me
and my own stupid acquiescence
this is adolescence, I think, squinting into indigo sea
as the girls with strappy sandals
strut, defying bunions and wolf whistles
their golden tans and giraffe necks
smooth in languor and pearls
whilst I, always comprised of irregular shape
ill measure and extreme emotion
suiting the addiction of smoking
and *Ricard Pastis* in art nouveau glass
one day I'll go home and he'll have met *that girl*
and I will have all the bills to pay

whilst summer hangs on in dribs and drabs
and calamine scabs turning brown
some last-minute rushing to throng the *Rue Meynadier*
I think I could go right now
turn my ankle, arch my eyebrow
invite a thin stranger to spread me over table for one
in hope I might feel something
more than the eclipse of youth
burning in Frankish sun.

Youth fits first into infinity

Inside is out
intent torn through
even children sleep sounder
even moons
even you

we learn to dance young
place our feet in tight shoes
cross our legs
hope nothing gets through

and still
mad hours arch away
the ochre beat of earthy things
where earwig and caterpillar roam
lethargic on dew
unseen horrors brew like old tea
staining the edges of tomorrow's bride

will this spider eat away
its web?
As youth fits first into infinity
then back again to rot
shall the unsaid follow you?
To a place without light
where wings are forbidden lusts
fallen shapes merge thoughts
chalky and immobile against
half-consumed ache?

perhaps
and perhaps come morning
rectified order will reign
a polite sterility regained
smearing dream with heavy neglect
and tossing nightmares
fat with play
back inside our heads.

Who then has the right?

Sometimes
though it is considered selfish, to think of self
to complain or feel, unease with one's burden
when all the children who die; tsunami, earthquake, starvation
have no recourse
conscience says; do not complain of your lot in life
sometimes despite this and the many boons
inherited in your comfortable life
of first world nation and running water
without hunger in the same impoverished way
sometimes, despite this
a voice within says; this feels so wrong
even though lucky compared to 80 percent of the world
there are days we seek to cry out; pain is in different forms
for the starving it is their belly
for the homeless, their houseless heads
for the exploited, safety that never comes
and for myself
fed twice a day, and able to turn on the heating when it gets cold at night
it is the knowing of all I have
and the pain that still persists
a hole within pulled apart
by all I know and all I cannot change
by the little pains that may
be ridiculed and said to be of no import
I would say this: everyone's brand of suffering counts
even the bored housewife at her therapist appointment
bemoaning the loss of her figure, the diminishment of her marriage
we are perhaps facile, shallow souls
only certain sufferings are truly considered worthy of mention
but for most of us who do not die of hunger, or live in war-torn continent
there are other forms of starvation and war
the child who stops eating, because her parents' divorce
so many who would be scorned for their reasons
this makes me saddest of all; the idea of permission to grieve
levels of what is deemed 'bad' versus 'weak'—judged for how we feel
when nobody, nobody but ourselves, knows or can compare

the pain of a child with everything in the world who STILL feels despair
and one who has never known anything
for pain is not as simple as contrasting suffering
it lies within us, folded and unfolded
depending on season of day and
temper of mind and much as we are told
shake it off, don't you know how lucky you are?
This can lead us into greater misery, for the worst pain
is the kind nobody thinks, has a right.

Servants of their tempest

The Japanese woman
out of girlhood one day
is robed and washed
painting herself in chalk
and cyanide
shaving her scalp
binding her tongue
brushing her teeth black
opens her mouth to receive
the urge of him
and he is small like a jackal
reminding her of monkey puzzle trees
abusing in figurative
the fragile cherry blossoms
dying on teak
beneath her and above, the world colors
and outcome saturates in ink
salvaged from the bottom of the sea
a squid relents and gives up his darkness
for all who create beauty
destroy the servants
of their tempest.

Imprint

Remove from wall
leaving mark, imprint of hang
representations of time
spent

behind remains a yellowed shadow
where the weight of images lay
observant of passing
fingers raised and smudging
reflecting glass on hours
grown and sewn

before too long, coats are no longer
piled on hook, shoes left, cased in mud
and outdoor pursuit
less the tick of days, more the semblance
as growing up, they scatter like milkweed
still the images stay mindful of
all that has passed, in good solid
anchor

when our pictures are lifted
finally, from their placement
retaining, an echo of this house
footsteps growing up in and from
launching out into fabric
wound in reels of trailing silk
as electricity retains
memory of our vimina presence in
absent nerve fire

we who briefly walk earth and
capture moments in daub of paint
and photograph, we who frame
memories to linger as outline on
soft plaster, holding up our
belief we count, exist beyond

flesh and water, some continuum of
passing, caves stained with petroglyph
retaining raw hang of us
speaking inaudibly after we are gone
and others lift to remove
who we were from
once crowded
walls.

Greco

Standing on tiptoe
other voices sounding angry, red background
your skin clammy to touch
infiltrate of heat and liquor
tasting your tongue
no need to buy my own drink
you reached around my waist
a thimble and a willow
blood surging in our veins
wild horses without stoppage
a pulse somewhere, rose high like music
your eyes were drawn downward
grief like modern art, disarticulate Greco
chin too long like a musical instrument
nose irregular and broken
your lips were thorns, whetted with scarlet
I saw only the urge of ourselves
cymbals crashing against high tide
dirt under our nails, knots in our hair
when love was violent in
its disregard for all
that is artificial.

As tightly we spindle faith

There are sinews of unsaid moments
trailing sweat stains
across best intentions
and girls who didn't unknot their tongues
plying their bellies full of seed
to assuage their threaded hunger
time paints lines on faces upturned
searching empty skies for sign of worth
as tightly we spindle faith, like
the cat who loses his game
in triangle of sunlight
with weary grasshopper
seeking shelter in
the dying of winter
collecting our bones
for kindling.

Not of man, not of woman

The earth cracked open
one ordinary thursday
thursday's child walked out
she has long to go

she asked her stand ins
but they were only cardboard
they could not nurture
or answer

setting out on foot
zola budd
if she swam oceans in seal fat
and ate stones to give her
some brevity
that was between her
and the cracks

once, crossing river
she saw herself reflected
her skin green like deep forest
with shallow scoop, she spoke to silver fish
telling them of her beginning
in clay too hard for shape

at night, skies were ringed with violet effleurage
swaths of fading red and night
cacophony, slued in warm air
she ate damsons and young grass
and bathed in fringes of wet brown mud, creeping from sleeping river
as sun crested, baking even, the patterns of life
her sleep grew in sync with form's outline
written on the shore
not of man
not of woman
far to go.

Whole

Wick the blade
sharp on stone
hoist stilled carcass
no more milk
furled on tanner's apron
stained auburn
slough death impulse
practice makes perfect
perfectly certain you bring with you
whole and formed
a way out of dividing yourself
piece by piece, slab by slab
until meat you are
lost from touch, butcher by default
sealed and bagged, sold by the pound
satiating others hunger
dormant in sacrifice
when did you lose the right
to be whole?

Bulimia

Hunger is a divinity
looking for worship
thirst a palace
empty of believers
her stomach rumbles
urging her to consume
last morsel
in her greed, she is full
in her abstinence, she is emptied
the mirror
licks her wounds
with echoes of those who stood
watching for signs
they can control
anything of their
world.

Elocution

I learned respect
from people who didn't pull punches
or back down
when fires were lit
they could be rude, acerbic
you could rely on their strength
they didn't change their mind
like channels or suffer from
indifference or inattention
nor would they pander
to popular schematic
theirs was an iron fist
scaring me into obedience
growing into respect
now I ask the same in return
or has decency
up and left?

The arsonists dilemma

Everything has to be memory
atoning
close the door quietly
catskills
high arches of ballet dancer
we are dead
walking grandly in symphony swell
open the gates
send in flowered chorus
temptation is a reddened cremation, vivid in foreign soil
they ask for you
diaphanous
stepping on ether
louder, louder
drown out
any distraction
here comes consequence
starched on rollers
vetting purity through strainers
thick with seaweed

state your truth
rocking in utterance
sharing apace, our vibrations
don't ask me why
addiction hisses on hot pavement
smoke makes memory vague, in lessening guilt
behind the patter, in urgency of rain sipping on ozone
we are imminent in entreaty
don't thirst for clarity
as punching fruit bites through glass, we deliver tulips lying naked in hotel
    rooms

the arsonist ate theologies for breakfast
wound twine around his middle fingers and pulled tight, when focusing
don't blink rapidly, they'll see, those liked girls who wore tutus and combat
    boots, cherished grief in ripe fog chasing figs

snow fell suddenly, draping concrete in fantastic doubtless gown, undersides of beauty, turn them over, both become nightmare, dove has claws, woman's maw, dark cave sucking you back, breathe through pleasure, swimming in fabrication

we smoked red feathers over hot coals and when he knelt to poison our glad hearts, we reveled in his attention

we, who will ourselves against stained spindle, unusable for grief; we who slowly turn toxic in transformation

hold on to sadness long throughout, ink permeates escaping with emboldened luster, licks our waiting vessel

it is possible to protect the abuser, too tightly we clasp what we know, even when it lashes us to ribbons

release
pain
watch it
acknowledge you and set sail
while firm in forgiven fund
we are once again weightless
burdening none by sorrow.

Show me yours, I'll show you mine

Time captured in jars, ready to unwind. They said you looked like Lana del Ray but she could be your aborted daughter. Rinsing down public toilets with bank notes, Lincoln's condemnation in empty fever, would be a solace as daylight is scorched for eternal night, he comes then to claim his payment, give me thirty brands of silver for your first born and a little bend over, don't make a fuss, be a good girl, here's a picture of your future, snap, her neck wears heavy chains, keep me upright in the red corridor sitting in pensioner pity, will we ever go home? When doors leading back, are as broken as we?

The Pitbull & the girl (part of the #unsung series)

Diane whipple
jogging all 100 pounds
returning home to quiet neighborhood
breathing in fresh sea air, san francisco harbor
sounds of boats and ferry bells
an unease in the wind
somewhere an unfamiliar sound
heavy chain collar clinking, a beige ear pricks up
watches in taut position, haunches tight and hot
steady dragging eyes, slowly observe
her hastening thin form, keys out, catch light and shine
sweat, her heavy breath, slap of sneakers on stairs

the creep in your neck
nails scratch on tarmac
fixing on fragile vein
she's 5'5, the female dog
taller, heavier, built for one bite, one lunge
powerful jaws, clamp
savagery in an instant
splash; blood everywhere
hardly time to scream
over before it began
keys fall, into scarlet

they found her fading
fallen in her own slick red
her throat destroyed
unable to speak
she beseeched with fading eyes
"tell her i love her"
not enough time
like a rag tossed aside
metaphor for how many times
diane didn't have to die.

Renesha McBride (part of the #unsung series)

In the motor city
renesha 19, broke down on dark street
disoriented, tired and afraid
she follows light through night
a house with bright porch
small girl, no working phone
knocks

from behind his fortress
theodore, the unbrave, feared … *what?*
A girl could break down his double doors?
Never considering her fear genuine
lost in night, no one in sight
he raised his shotgun, sighted the shot
aimed straight for her head
your honor it was self-defense!
I feared for my life!
sitting watching porn in the middle of the night

a weaponless girl chose the wrong house
he saw her black skin, snap judgment
she's breaking in!
To rob me! I'll show her!
My home is my castle
behind law he stood certain
nobody would see race was why
renesha mcbride died that day

the jury didn't agree
he's doing time in a 6 x 3
but how does it bring her back?
Why didn't people march about that?
He gunned her down, because she dared
to assume compassion lay
on the other side
and not a man seething
with excuses to fire.

Hard drinker

Don't hold me so close
I'm made of coffee
in water I dissolve
only to taste bitter
and you'll want
more than I can fill.

Fracture

When you teach a child to grit its teeth against unacceptable things
when you tell it to sit afterward at a table, like nothing happened
you engender a child who carries broken
the ill-made breakage of their soul
fractured against despair
for that child
will never tell
It shall boil inside
like an oven without off switch
and one day that child will hurt someone
for all the years of secrets
It might be toward another person
or they may just cut the wires
holding them up.

Hollywood

I suppose it's cruel to tell you
your posture is bad
you don't do the fine clothes you wear justice
your spine is bent and you hold your stomach in
but the bulge of your conscience belies best attempt
at smoothing down, gaping seams
where sewn in and stuffed, you appear to
crawl out and long for release
I suppose it's cruel to tell you
whilst your roots don't show, your feet are muddy
your lipsticks crooked, like you found your hands
at the bottom of a well and pulling them up with
your teeth, you chipped your smile and smudged your
mouth, trying to fix them back in time for
the camera lights coming on at six.

For the wasps to feast

Three hours
unflinching on eiderdown, turning cream pages
sound of cat lifting window screen, bending in yogic form
escaping house in black and white yawn
to hunt marigold-colored birds
making paper cut-out shadows of themselves, against dangling feeder

the cat does not know, next year he will be sleeping
underneath dry earth and meal himself
for worm and bug, or how his life is precious
not to hunted bird, mocking his arthritic play
but the hands feeding him every night
stroking his aches, dreaming of ways
to make whole, what is incomplete

so long as we know death, we know pain
we know joy, we know the value of moments
spread out like jam, for the wasps to feast
both bitter and sweet.

(For Halo)

Notions

Failed faces in family portraits
abducted in lure
climb the leaf strewn stairs
obliterated stone step blanketed in autumn fall
red, gold, colors of death and grandeur
wear our victimhood high on neck to obliterate scar
trees still weighted with sap hold their burdens, like young girls with fans and
    dance cards
released where? Back into the wild
finding footing
attachment in deferred chill
motherhood
I never connected to notions of family
coiled in dresses train, streaming coming storm
come home
before night fall.

Until it's lost

65-year-old glad rag with orange perma tan
works beach front with gin drinking hands
ratty thinning hair grown long, wearing bright shirts short
belly strains against yeasty beer bulge
he's not really a painter, he's more of a sand waiter
watching the girls go by, with one hand down faded underwear
40-year wife looks 32 with Xanax dissatisfaction
scratching the yoke of middle-age with regular tweaks
long neck producing nasal vowels, elongating to silent scream
she wore a square hat when they married, and his eyes lit up
now they glaze like maraschino cherries in whiskey sours
taking in the rocky waves breaking shore
over thorns their honeymoon broke beds, settled down into quiet discontent
slack mouthed he observes 18-year-old red-head
with ginger eye lashes and flat chest strut by
deep mahogany girls with tight cornrow and buttered cheeks
giving him the stink eye
his sullen dislike of his wife's saddle thighs starved into a size 2 dress
lest he protest or compare
she'd like to ask; what does he really want to eat?
What does he really want when he divides up his greed?
They sit around small stuffy table with empty people
talking themselves up like false fire, forgetful anything is astonishing
their mediocrity a faded pattern with pockets full of non-vocalized questions
the only provocateur, entitlement, ground on spit for all to carve
they are dull, those who breathe thin air and shallow lusts
he doesn't yet know the 18-year-old will suck him off
pick his pocket, and steal his grandfather's watch
later on, when his wife finds out she's got cancer
she leaves the door open, he can buy a new lock
for an empty box, because nobody knows what they have
until it's lost.

Overboard

There in the enfolding quiet pallor of morning
there against the redness of chain tugging at your neck
there in pushing against encasement, a seed within a nut, knocking
for release

still time has bidden us wait, hold this pattern, trace the lines of your making
still day has glimmered over rosewood mountains, dissolved in thought
still tomorrow may not permit entry, in low slung neck we bow, players of
dull coin

this moment there is only the urge for formation, granting hope in egg-shell
this feeling of heaviness, a spell, a shackle, a bracelet of thorns, some shallow
    divined source
this need to clamber back into light, spilling like a lover, against unreachable place
in lusty splay

of time our sorrow ribbons memories, would we lose our source, and wake afresh
    again
of escape, we dream, to be anything but the anchor, caught in deep weeds, rusting
    beneath
calm surface, finding fire, lest it quenches release, rise again, higher toward yourself

floating against current
brandished by direction
half-submerged drinking in
oceans temperate nature
give me your unyielding hour
to smooth against burning brow
that I might remove torment
plucking it like unwanted past
thrown overboard.

Artists model

The artist who was never an artist
painted the model who was never a model
he bragged bloatedly about her pedigree
because his own fused brush was in some doubt
whilst the girl who wasn't beautiful and
wished instead for love
posed with her legs spread and her back arched
hoping in render
she would be cherished
as in life
she never was.

Cauchemar

The young dog pulled the old woman
too fast on his leash
she fell and bruised her knees
supplicant in grass noticing
how it felt to be uncomfortable
when for long days she forgot herself
in the warm steam of pots, pans and the
gentle hum of life washing away
it is good to recall why
to wonder if we are awake
and what of this world we can still effect change
too much comfort dulls our edges
we find ourselves slipping quiet into a full bath of sleep
no longer questioning things the way as hot adolescents
we railed and roared into the sounding void
still, we must persist if we wish to wake from dream
finding a world, not a nightmare
grazing beneath our window.

Pain

You were never fashionable
liked turning up late and unattended
you wore your clothes a little downturned
shabby at the heels, giving yourself away
by the chip of your paint and the extent of your fray
Pain
you were never invited to the party
given a pretty dress to hide your scars reaching
over neckline like dancers hosting spectacle
gloves to disguise the wring of your chaffed hands
or dark glasses to block out sadness inking your eyes
tears are not required to show the world your grief
just look beneath the cover
you will see if you want to see
Pain
nobody wanted to visit so you grew around the door
knob and covered the lock, dark ivy, stopping anyone knowing
someone fitful murdered inside
a clock without hands, a three-legged stool and straining
ankle attempting to tie rope to ceiling beam
you swing
Pain
slow as air in warm room
rising
they did not want your sorrow
so, you stilled the knife
carving you into slices
rebuked crisscross art
flowers in rosette
swing low
a bloom
without
perfume.

Wait

I'm going to tell you something you don't want to hear
grief is a sticky substance
it gets underneath, where the light goes and sucks it out
feels like metal touching the roof of your mouth, releasing soreness
invading peace with tender fingers, reaching in for our hope
I wake up, alone, you're not there
you're on a monitor, in a bed, with lights blinking out
a window, a life built and dismantled, just that fast
helicopter taking off launching pad, making everything unstable
flying to bring us salvation, but what of us? Lost on the wind
beneath moons we sung each other's feathers full
time slowing down in favor, a kindness bestowed by naivety
I tell myself, today is not the day I will fall, become enveloped in grief
my heart argued long to feel goodness not sorrow
then I think of you, *mon ciel étoilé,* slipping away, more inside my head
than here in this pulsing world, as easily shut off as a machine unable to
bring you back whole, illness is a dancer in reverse
I danced with you once, we moved across ugly floors as if diamonds were
    beneath us
two young things high on life, not knowing we were disintegrating, memories
    rusting
our house, feels so empty without your movement, in night we rubbed
    imperceptibly
you slept like a child and I didn't know, all those years I wanted a child, I had
    you
held close to my chest, hoping my heart would suffice to reanimate and keep
    you safe
I couldn't heal you my love; I couldn't save you my love
we spun away from the other, like dust swept up and discarded
neither knowing it would become, an impossible reality
you lie more still than I feel, harpooned by failing health
once your eyes so beautiful now betray the fatigue of looking too closely
and I sit
thinking one day
I will write and you will not

reply
you will never respond and
I
will always
wait.

Late bloom

The late bloom of woman
is my favorite perfume
when young it is easy to pass
soft clear skin, long straight limbs, no time to
gather brambles in your skirt or tar on your feet
you run nimble and unraveled like
free wool released from snare
re-made lost rabbit foot, the fleet
of heart, dashing across snow to sleep beneath thin frost
you are unburdened by life, a green elm
bending in time to tapered rhythm
as cantaloupe sun sets on your forehead
the light changes and makes unkind patterns of use and toil
spoiling a little of your wonder
marking with concentration and hour
spent jarring days in keep
some damson, some cherry, some apricot
all hues of us, avoiding spoil, danger in our fermenting sweetness
look closer, past obvious cues of bruised tips and worn knees knelt in
giving others, their day in the sun
lift the child, make him whole
feed him milk from tendered breast
the mother, the keeper of secrets
wound in fable around her fingers, like rings from each life
enriching her, gentle as night breeze
gathering her skirts high, catching no thorns
she knows how best to avoid the worn lament of loss
her heart shored against familiar kinds of pain
and better for her concavity
scooped as rich as coffee grain, redolent in their promised taste
she is turning toward luminosity, her eyes wide and open
let the world in
let her translate you
with her rooted draught of beauty
her long-lived sorrow, like depression era glass prized most

for evoking and enduring
her hands are strong and know not
how to release or let down
those who need her strength and her
proffering depth.

Frenzy

The dial on the pressure cooker wasn't yet turned to scald

her feathers nonetheless were falling pitifully without need of pluck, revealing emptiness

first eyebrows, then bashful hairline, see through scalp shocked in pink and mottle

who knew beneath our sum, a solar deprived effigy resided?

Biding time till crone-hood, too soon too soon, slippered and calcified came?

Her dresses fit her snug, her burgeoning waist-line swelled like plaster-cast parachute

thinning all over, skin, nails, lips, vision, tongue

briefly she thought of the Italian man who wished to do a head transplant

and how it would feel to inhabit a body of one and twenty

rather than the snubbing betrayal of figuring youth turning old before count of time

whitening hair like skeletal cats' whiskers, sticking vertically out in fain mockery

breasts losing volume wilt, mind's edge growing numb, forgetful, succumb, succumb

her misbehaving womb, her unapologetic ovaries, plunging menopausal cavort

all her friends still suckling their children, warming up tins of pureed carrots and apple

while she aged ahead of the mirror, chipping away pieces like a chalky cliff, beset by angry sea

since when did we grow crooked, gnarled and tired, peeing in the night like a wraith?
It was fortunate nobody witnessed her decay, fortunate she'd sewn her sag away

in a bento box for *not yet, not yet, oh no here it comes*, the fury of vengeful dying hormones

flurrying like hot faced dancers in front of flickering stage lights posed in O, *Oh not now!*

Heat burning her thighs, soaking sheets, holding the ocean within all these years, then sweating out into shame-faced night

a chorus of finches wake her in the mauve morning, still bleary-eyed and stiff, can this be it?

Old age before prescription, get ready, throw away your dreams for conveyor-belt ageism

she goes to the white-wash store, and the pierced young man behind over-priced coffee counter says;

you're looking beautiful as ever, what have you done? Your cheeks are so full and auburn!

She laughs like a mad woman, knitting her cart in splendid lurch, splashing hot coffee on her hastily thrown on shirt

this world is mad, and we walk among it, nobody knowing, we're half mad too, surely a delusion, a fine dream, a web

an unexpected laugh, and there she is again, staring into water, echoing back, ready to chase herself through fields

teaming with late flowers, mindful of their curtsey at night, and their full heads of clover bewitching sleepy bees to frenzy.

Aren't You?

when
the thick trunk of families, surges upward and onward
and the line thins out of impatient elbows
you stand as you always have
alone
more conscious of their abundant overflow
at an airport without a ticket, watching throngs of souls
connected and coming together, like migration encourages the swell and surge
    of birds riding warm air
somehow knowing, they are part of a greater collective
and you stand there, in your well-worn shoes
and your empty pockets ache, for someone to turn and say

aren't you with us?

Pirate Radio

Totems she left behind

what lost?

What gained?

Cinereal clouds pierce Cimmerian dusk

your fingers fastening in my hair

we interlace in one another

le plus vieux pont, la plus jeune émotion

lineament of women,

crossing from mortal to sempiternal

drawing you to me, redolent with love-making

I empty myself inside you, like flowers plucked will dry

and retain their incense

your neck a budding posy of marble obsidian, onyx, malachite, rose quartz

pillowed thighs, yielding beneath entreaty

a woman is nectar, ambrosia, a mist on the breath of dusk

her center a temple to invoke

donne-moi ta soif laissez-moi vous rassasier

entreat the reciting of capture till we ripen into rapture

wordless in renewal, you lend me promise

I bestow the eternal endeavor turning metal dial,

through tempest comes outlying supplication of wireless reverie

Dormir sous les vagues

it's 1999 again and we're drying our wet socks on hot radiators,

the tips torn by exertion, our fingers

chill-blain, curling mouths open to each other

fais-moi pleurer de plaisir like blind seals

dipping beneath ocean coming up for air

as fire crackles across pirate radio wave.

Suddenly it is midnight on the water

I leave a stain on my letter to you, with the tinny ring of my mug
tea left cold when you called and I ran out
following your voice like a siren, heedless of consequence
you are the devour of my hesitation, I hesitate never when you call
side-stepping consequence like a brothel, seeking your presence as a sinner
looks for absolution and a saint kneels until it hurts, my ache is so
deeply laid it could not be recovered, even if they brought chains
here, streets bleed violet in shuttered neon blink
nights deepest scold rests

we take the ferry out into pelagic wake
afloat on silence, illumination veiled
your forearms, muscular against thin wrists
beneath sturgeon moon we shift like light
particulate drawn by shivering lodestone
time, her death-and-gloried face
far flung from our observance, no more
liturgy of unspoken entreaties

there are no other words for your mouth
it is placed on your face like a torment, a
famine to touch, never stop craving, its perfect shape

suddenly it is midnight on the water, my body
sore from your touch, we watch in hush
dark silhouettes take on life
their grave countenance
caught briefly by moon peel
as glossy as the pearl of your face
incandescent as we pass by

our hands entwined
we may be invisible compared to
the rest, but here, here we
exist

Amulet

No they didn't write poems about you and they didn't write poems about me
they didn't write poems about us
we were a label, a provocation, pornography
perhaps sometimes a curse, misfortune
something to deride in that lazy way
people who find it amusing to poke fun, do
I imagine them now
sipping on over-sweet lemonade in lawn chairs
pointing when we pass by
if younger they might say
"well those two probably look good doing it"
but as we're past the sell by date of women
they stay with the flabby slurs, the ways of erasure
subtle and time tested
"those damn lesbians I bet they are
protesting-to-gain-attention-and-notoriety-again
won't-they-just-quit-trying-to-queer-the-world"
(I wonder what they DO in bed?)
the jokes about too many cats, why don't we have short hair
or wear wife-beaters (was that ever really a thing?)

it could be 1950 (but then we'd be arrested)
it could be 1975 (but then we'd just be beaten and raped)
it could be 1990 (dirty looks on the street, possibly pity)

I remember a friend asking me why I hadn't been attracted to her
as if being a lesbian made me a predator and ready for anyone
it could be tomorrow and you're let go at your job but you can't prove why
despite your boss being a Christian Scientist
the newspaper has an article on gay commitment ceremonies
why gays shouldn't push the envelope, they make it worse (by existing?)
you bring in the post, we still can't marry though a
colleague got drunk hitched to a girl he knew 24 hours last weekend in Vegas
we still can't immigrate which is why I don't drive and I work
two badly paid illegal jobs and don't answer our phone
if you get sick, your family will block me from visiting or living in my own
    home

we laugh they would even take the cat (can't you queer a cat?)
my friend who is a Catholic, asks me why gay-marriage is
so important, after all it's not illegal to be gay anymore what
else do you really need? She married her high school sweetheart (but it's
    different, how?).
I need to feel safe, equal, legitimized; your aunt once asked
why the law changing would achieve that, and we considered
her own 3 marriages and children and had no words
a collar of intolerance imposed by the majority
that feels like half warm water choking your right to live free.
"At least it's not illegal anymore," a teacher said, almost consolidatory
as if she knew what that felt like, or the wick of fear seeing police
lights in your rear-view mirror, (and one of them is COLORED the lead cop
said before asking us to place our hands on the car and assume the position)
When the law changed and the signs that said;
marriage equals a man and a woman NO queers! Were removed
the neighbors asked us if we were going to get married
have a big party in the back garden, they would ask their cousin to make a
    rainbow cake
the smile on my face felt tight
like when you put spray on sun lotion and it dries in place
because all the grief carried around had become our children
all the fear had become our legacy, we were tired of explaining anything
or even attempting to be part of straight people's trending celebrations
for finally possessing rights
it seemed easier then
to just carry on being the way we always had been
trying to avoid detection
like it had been an amulet, whether we wanted it or not
that took us through the darkness, until we
no longer needed the light.

The unseen world

At the corner of your mouth, where it curls in gentle disdain, a little spiting mirth; lives the unseen world

In your eyes, polished obsidian run through with black onyx, lies the hearth of your internal combustion

As you breathe, I cannot fail to notice the lovely juxtaposition of your bones gleaming beneath apricot skin, as the buttons on your shirt attest, each breath yawning her fitful glimpse

I cannot help but wonder those stored bottles of delight, high upon your shelf, how your nipples would taste, the flowered breath of your heart of palm

And divining center, that pulsing mandala, reaching her fragrance into dreamworld, the color of aubergine and hibiscus bled in winter river, as redwood is lost to time

My artichoke girl, wreathed in wild flowers, your body a temple for this supplicant, as light diminishes, your thirsty form grows spectral, a mango tree heavy in fruiting

From within, you glow with the hardy tempest of your nature, a pulsing, feckless creature, nimble in your art of deft possession

If I could starve for want of you, I believe I would. For no moment passes with satisfaction, unless in some way, you exist on its marble periphery

The very yoke of a day is cast by your presence. I could subsist on the rounding detour of your thighs for a hundred sleepless nights

Grow from your slumber the memories of your cries, curled in my ear, my lips, my reincarnation of our slippery motion to capture

When it is cold my hands seek your bright match to kindle animation, climbing from the solace of you, strengthened by remembered, evoked echo of intimacy

A song wound around my ribs as river reeds pull the charmed to their divine drowning and with last sip of air, we relinquish control and let go

My love; your eyes bewitch my life blood, kindling the charred rejoinder of hope, a poppet to your sorcerery, emerging from deep forest

When dying comes for me, it'll be your face I kiss, feverish and familiar, your preternatural smile haunting my passage, faithful ghost, mine

For some there is no method of separation, we are bound in crushed roses to one

In this place. In each other. A languid, yawning soft space between; the unseen world.

Acknowledgements

Indie Blu(e) Publishing: Christine E. Ray. Kindra M. Austin. Vic Manzi.

Borderless Journal: Mitali Chakravarty.

The Pine Cone Review: Susmita Paul and Dr. Khusi Pattanayak.

BlackBird Press: Mira Hadlow.

Parcham: Shayan A. Bhowmik

Tribe: Ava & H, Mark, Susi, Tre, Chuck, Crystal, Meg, Johann, Emily, Leah, Jack, Diane, Monique, Danny, Nicole, Megha, Renee, Raili, Didi, Joaquin, Rachel, Hanlie, Susie, Sun, Clayton, Anthony, Marjorie, Nicholas, Hanna, Louise, Philip, Dustin, Matt & Jen, Joslyn, Heather, Kavita, Ruth & Shin, Mel & Tony, Nadia, Sarah, Amita, Velma, Zilka, Jaime.

WordPress: Peter Aldino, Betty Albright, John Biscello, Jill Mason Blake, Susi Bocks, Tara Caribou, Jane Dougherty, Rob Goldstein, Shweta Rao Garg, Em, Helena, Holly, Annette Kalandros, Erik Klingenberg, Derrick Knight, Tremaine Loadholt, Aakriti Kuntal, Linda Paul, Georgia Park, Rob Plath, S. A. Quinox, Christine Renney, Merril Smith, Tony Single, Megha Sood, Eric Syrdal, Andrew McDowell, Monique Moore, Devika Mathur, Angie Waters, Bob Wertzler, Laurie Wise, Philip Andrew Wardlow, Lamarr Wenrich.

Deep gratitude to the incredible Kai Coggin, Tremaine Loadholt, Nicole Lyons, Robert Okaji, and Donna Snyder for your ARC reviews. I admire the heck out of you.

Deep appreciation for my book front & back covers by Maaike Pluym (IG: @poisonmikey). Interior moth illustration by Monochromier and image of masked fox-woman by Pintal Sari.

Thank you so much to Leah Maines, Christen Kincaid, and Finishing Line Press.

Finally, and most of all: My velvet ribbon. Without whom, I would unravel.

Candice Louisa Daquin is of Sephardi French/Egyptian descent. Born in Europe, Daquin worked in publishing for The U.S., Embassy / Chamber of Commerce before immigrating to the American Southwest to study and become a Psychotherapist, where she has continued writing and editing whilst practicing as a therapist. Daquin has worked at Jewish Community Centers and Rape Crisis Centers both in Texas and Ontario, Canada. Her area of specialization is adults sexually abused as children. Prior to publishing her own poetry collections, Daquin regularly wrote for the poetry periodicals: *Rattle* and *The Northern Poetry Review*. Daquin is Senior Editor at Indie Blu(e) Publishing, a feminist micro-press. Writer-in-Residence for *Borderless Journal*. Editor of Poetry & Art for *The Pine Cone Review*. Editor, for Blackbird Press.

Daquin's poetic work takes its form from the confessional women poets of the 19th and 20th century as well as queer authors writing from the 1950's onward. Her career(s) teaching critical thinking and practicing as a psychotherapist, have heavily influenced her work, with explored key themes including; sexual-abuse, parental-relationships, mental illness and queer-identity. Daquin's work is also significantly imprinted by Audre Lorde, Françoise Sagan, Angela Carter, activist Egyptian physician Nawal El Saadawi, Navdanya seed bank creator/campaigner Vandana Shiva, Pablo Neruda, Israeli PM Golda Mier, Toni Morrison and feminist philosophers bell hooks, Hélène Cixous and Luce Irigaray.

As a queer woman of mixed ethnicity and passionate feminist beliefs concerning equality, Daquin's poetry is her body of evidence.

Recent Poetry in Anthologies:
Heartstrings, (Authors Press, Ed. Sanjula Sharma)
Body Of Memories: A Collection of Memoirs & Personal Essays (Ed Lopamudra Banerjee)
Lilith—INNSÆI: International Journal of Creative Literature for Peace and Humanity
The Brown Critique "Home" Anthology (The Brown Critique)
Oxygen: Parables of Pandemic (River Paw Press)
Cuckoo In Crisis: 25 Women Poets (Akhand Publishing House)
Boundless 2021: The anthology of the Rio Grande Valley International Poetry Festival
Paws Healing the Earth, (River Paw Press)
Overcoming Fear: Based on true events (Wingless Dreamer)
The Poets Symphony: Verses, Melodies, and Lyrical Poems (Raw Earth Ink)
Texas Best Emerging Poets, (Z Publishing House)
All the Lonely People (Free Verse Revolution)
America's Emerging Poets 2018: West Region (Z Publishing House)

Recent Editor/Co-Editor of:
The Gift of Mercy, Annette Kalandros (2022)
Hospital Poems, Nancy Dunlop (2022)
Hungry for Ghosts, Kristin Kory (2022)
Girl on a Swing, D. B. Wright (2022)
Relative Traumas, Nadia Garofalo (2022)
But You Don't Look Sick: The Real Life Adventures of Fibro Bitches, Lupus Warriors and other Super Heroes Battling Invisible Illness (2021)
The Killing Holiday, Kindra Austin (2021)
Some Words Never Sleep, Zinia Mitra (2021)
Through The Looking Glass: Reflecting on Madness and Chaos Within (2021)
The Kali Project: Invoking the Goddess Within / Indian Women's Voices (2021)
As the World Burns: Writers and Artists Reflect on a World Gone Mad (2020)
Crimson Skins, Devika Mathur (2020)
Flowers on the Wall, Kristiana Reed (2020)
SMITTEN This Is What Love Looks Like: Poetry by Women for Women (2019)
Luminarium, Maria Gianna Iannucci (2019)
Dead's Haven (Olivia & Hale Book 3), Nicolas Gagnier (2019)
We Will Not Be Silenced: The Lived Experience of Sexual Harassment and Sexual Assault Told Powerfully Through Poetry, Prose, Essay, and Art (2018)

Own Poetry Collections:
Chapbooks: *The Bright Day Has Gone Child and You Are in for the Dark,*
Illusions of Existing, Sit in Fever.
A Jar for the Jarring (South Texas Press / Palpitate Press)
Pinch the Lock (Finishing Line Press)
Tainted by the Same Counterfeit (Finishing Line Press)

CANDICE

LOUISA DAQUIN

Lightning Source UK Ltd.
Milton Keynes UK
UKHW012123070223
416656UK00008B/94